MW01490279

<u>RACISM</u>

Recognizing the Anguish of Caustic Insensitivity and Senseless Mistreatment

A Black Lives Matter Proffering

by: Janne Jameson

Copyright 2020 by Janne Jameson

All Rights Reserved

*To the Prince of Peace and of every
precious promise,
I am eternally undeserving and grateful for Your
LOVE, FORGIVENESS, SALVATION and ARMS of
PROTECTION that never tire of carrying me,...ever.*

*To my amazing Mom and Dad, my "Ace" of a
Brother and my incredible Husband,
who collectively and individually bring to my life
what no one else can.*

Table of Contents:

*We're human. We all harbor Life's
preferences & minor dislikes;
THIS style, **THIS** flavor, **THIS** genre
over **THAT ONE**.
But, eliciting **HATRED** for the hue of
one's skin,
Abysmally fails to ever be a sufficient
REASON.*

Janne Jameson

◇ INTRODUCTION ◇

How does a parent shield a child from RACISM? Try as they might, children simply cannot be protected. Sooner or later, the *World* and its havoc will make its way into **'*their world.*'**

The story that follows is how RACISM made itself known to me,...how I failed to face it head on,...and the lessons I took away from it.

While these events in no way equal the deadly, demoralizing, detrimental, racially charged acts that have spawned the current **BLACK LIVES MATTER MOVEMENT**, they do reflect how one child's life was tainted forever by RACISM.

Perhaps it will encourage you to dredge up from the recesses of your mind,... just where it all began for you.

◇ CHAPTER 1 ◇

A SKATING PARTY,... my younger brother, who would later become more precious than platinum to me, and I were beyond excited! It was to be held after school on a Friday evening, Mom and Dad had given the 'ok' and we were all set. They had consented to let their two children rendezvous with their classmates for an inaugural outing at the local skating rink. We couldn't roller skate a lick, but since when does anything 'new' ever discourage kids?

Having received our parental admonishments to be mindful of each other's whereabouts, to exercise safety, to not leave with anyone except herself or Dad, and to call if there was an emergency, Mom dropped us off.

As the oldest sibling by 3 years, I pocketed the money she'd handed me for the evening to encompass our skate rental fees, snacks and a little extra for any unforeseen events.

The place was buzzing with a host of other kids, some older than my 8 years of age, some younger, some who owned their skates, and others, like us, who didn't. We spotted my friends from school at the door, and though unfamiliar with the layout, entered and made our way to stand in line to rent our skates. With the upbeat music already blasting, some skaters were expertly whizzing around the rink, others were just leisurely sitting on the benches lacing up their skates and happily conversing away. I turned my attention to the pricing board that hung above the counter while we waited. Calculating how much the rental of two sets of skates would cost, we inched ever closer to the counter.

"Skates for two, please." It was our turn, and I'd stepped forward to give, (let's refer to her as "Mrs. Q."), the number of my party and our sizes. I had noticed that she'd greeted me rather gruffly and seemed perturbed by our presence as if we'd committed some skating-rink-novice-faux-paus. I was quite sure we hadn't because I'd spent the last several minutes studying how the kids in line ahead of me were ordering their skates. I hadn't noticed Mrs. Q. being tight-lipped to them, but what did I know?

Someone retrieved our skates from the back wall of what must have been hundreds of pairs in every size imaginable. I handed her the money, passed my little brother his skates and waited for the monetary change. Still scowling, no hint of a smile, she pushed the money towards me and waited. As I counted the change, I froze. I recounted it. I looked back at the pricing board, re-calculating.

This wasn't correct; she had mistakenly *shortchanged* me almost $2.00. Finally, I looked back at her.

There was no misreading the, "I-dare-you-to-challenge-me-little-black-girl," HATRED in her adult eyes.

That's when 'shortchanged' elevated to being 'cheated'.

That's when RACISM made its grand entrance into my life.

I'd never really had it aimed at me like a weapon before, but I recognized it, and it was real.

I waited for her to make amends, to realize that I *knew* I hadn't been given the proper amount of change, to acknowledge that she'd "accidentally" cheated me. When she did nothing except continue to stare coldly at me, as if my very unintimidating 8 year old stature was an invasion to her universe, to my disillusionment, I closed my little fist around the money, picked up my skates, beckoned my brother to follow me...and walked away.

I did not speak up.

I did not refute her wrongful deed against myself and my brother, who had remained innocently oblivious to what had just transpired.

RACISM. Blatant-unprovoked-"what-did-I-do-to-you?..."-RACISM.

On the bench, I donned my skates and turned to my brother to help him tighten his laces, all the while proceeding to count, re-count, add and subtract figures, trying to justify Mrs. Q's racist actions.

I looked around. Why was there a skating rink full of kids who were skating for LESS than what my Mom had given us to do??

I knew how to count money. What had happened wasn't right, of that I was sure. I just didn't have the voice, the experience, the effrontery to confront the wrongdoing done unto us.

We managed to skate, (mostly pull-by-handrail), ourselves around for the rest of the evening. I could feel the money in my front right pocket. I calculated what I would need later for our concessions tab, and while I knew my evening was tainted, what I would soon grasp was that my life was now scarred by RACISM.

I'd withered under the pressure to call out a racial injustice directed at me and my sibling.

My brother and I later refreshed ourselves with snacks, (the correct change was given this time, albeit by a different employee), and all too soon the skates were returned, sneakers were re-tied,...and Mom was waiting.

◇ CHAPTER 2 ◇

"Maybe she won't count the money," I thought. "Perhaps she won't even ask about it at all."

We rode home that night chit-chatting lightly about the songs we'd heard, the friends we'd laughed with and the skating skills we thought we'd honed over the course of just a few hours. Shortly after arrival, we relayed the same account of our evening with Dad; they were both pleased that we'd had a great time, or "seemed" to have had, in my case. With instructions to prepare to go to sleep, I heard Mom's voice from down the hall before she appeared in the doorway.

"By the way, do you have my change?" she asked, matter-of-factly.

My delusion that tonight's exposed weakness to handle the racial inside-curveball that I'd been clipped on the kneecaps with was splintered like an old wooden bat .

"Yes Ma'am," I answered warily. (There was no "Yep, Yeah or Uh-huh" response in our household when addressing my parents. Ever.)

Years later, I would come to develop a fascination with Sir Arthur Conan Doyle's fictional character at 221B Baker Street, with his famous Deerstalker Hat, stylish Iverness Cape and Calabash Pipe. Doyle's written works notwithstanding, this mentally fascinating sleuth, in my opinion, has been portrayed to a tee by any number of devoted actors, with high praises lavished on the Disney Animated version entitled: "The Great Mouse Detective", in which Disney pays tribute to actor Basil Rathbone's 1939 investigative talents by naming London's most famous detective, "Basil of Baker Street",...who plays the violin with great aplomb, possesses all the loveable panache and swagger you could hope for and whose nemesis, "Professor Ratigan", voiced chillingly as only Vincent Price could, is not to be missed. (Tyler Perry, I'd volunteer for any role if you would please craft a version starring an African American actor.)

I'd left her money on the nightstand, and even as I directed her to it, watched her pick it up and count it, I knew the moment I'd dreaded, since I'd turned away with cowardice from the HATE-filled eyes of Mrs. Q. at the register, was upon me.

She looked at me.

As I lived and breathed, before my very eyes, she turned into the female persona of Sherlock Holmes.

Sher(y)l-ock Holmes.

With her Mother's-221B-Baker-Street-Methodology, she calculated and deduced the events of the evening as if she had shadowed us the entire time without our knowledge. (It was, after-all, *elementary, my dear Janne.*) She did Doyle's London Detective proud,...very proud indeed.

"How much did I give you?"
"How much was admission?"
"How much did you spend on concessions for the two of you?"

Deeply ashamed, I answered her. The indurated pit in my stomach that I'd been harboring for hours could not be ignored.

"So, where is the rest of it, Janne?" she further inquired.

"I don't have it. I didn't receive it from the cashier," I meekly replied.

By this time, we'd acquired a small audience as my Dad had sauntered in the room, and my brother was present, too. "What happened?" Dad asked.

Forever etched in my mind's eye is Mom pinning me with the most abject look of disappointment, simmering ire and unavoidable truth. Gaze still locked on me, she answered Dad by stating to me, "You let her cheat you."

Dad was appalled. My brother looked sorrowfully at me.

It was getting late. What followed was not so much what I deserved, but what I needed. No, it wasn't a spanking; although, in hindsight, that would've hurt much less. 'Parenting' is what followed. At the end of a long Friday, on the heels of what must have been an even longer work week, where they faithfully and unselfishly worked to provide for their two children's private Christian School education, food, shelter, clothing, books, toys and recreation,...they did what they were called to do in that moment and parented us.

Being African American, they explained, is enough to make some members of other races in this world see us as a target. Mrs. Q. was Caucasian and happened to be one of those people. I had to use my voice for Truth. They said that it was my "responsibility" to make sure that I and my brother were being treated fairly. It was incumbent upon me to respectfully bring to light what I felt was a racial injustice masquerading as a mistake. You cannot just ignore RACISM; it's a very real entity that will come for you time and again if you allowed it.

I apologized and felt awful that I'd taken their trust and tossed it away. Mom switched off the light; I lay down and turned towards the wall in the darkness. My shame still shone bright, though. I thought about what they had said and felt that I'd botched tonight's outing by treating the Green $$$ of my Black parents as if it was worth less than the White parents' Green $$$ that lay in that same cash register.

Then, I got angry.

On one hand, my Mom had confirmed that my mental mathematic skills were correct. On the other hand, I had allowed myself to be cheated at the age of 8 years old. I'd been accosted by RACISM and I'd allowed it to wipe its feet on my back. I hadn't spoken up, hadn't used my voice to make the racial prejudice audible. I'd embarrassed my parents, and myself. I'd set a bad example for my brother. I'd allowed an adult Caucasian, a perfect stranger to take advantage of my youth and inexperience in handling racial bias.

This wasn't right.

I KNEW better; my parents DEMANDED, and my brother DESERVED better from me. My teachers, who were Caucasian up until that point and had treated me no differently than my Caucasian classmates, EXPECTED better.

I assured myself of one thing that night while looking towards a wall that I couldn't see but knew was there,...NEVER AGAIN.

NEVER. AGAIN.

NEVER AGAIN would I allow someone to cheat me, or worse yet my family, intentional or not, Caucasian or not.

If this was a facet of RACISM, a gemologist's polishing cloth would be utterly useless in removing the indelible tarnish on this dense, overly abundant stone.

Evidently, it wasn't obligated to overtly present itself as I'd seen on Alex Haley's TV mini-series: ROOTS. That eye-opening portrayal of the unlawful, unapologetically brazen, disgustingly sinful and brutal mistreatment of Black Slaves, had left me bristling with resentment when I'd watched alongside my family, Mom and Dad explaining the scenes that were difficult for us to comprehend at our ages. Lying there wide awake, I recalled the horrifying images of the insults, the inhumane living quarters, the bloody whippings, the back-breaking labor in unbearable heat, the incessant half-starved conditions, the unparalleled fear of knowing that your life was inferiorly valued to the *canines that had been sicced to hunt* **you** *down like the animals* **they** *were*,...all to have it culminate in the sheer terror of being lynched.

NEVER. AGAIN.

What I discovered as I grew, was that RACISM is indeed a sleepless, multi-headed beast that doesn't mind where, when or through whom it rears its scornful, derogatory traits.

◇ CHAPTER 3 ◇

I've often wondered since that night what Mrs. Q. at the skating rink taught her kids. Caucasian though she was, she was still a bit older than my parents, so it wasn't likely that I'd ever come across her kids at my grade level. So, what was it that sparked her instant dislike of me, and to an extended degree, my brother? Did she feel a deeper satisfaction when she'd fed her children breakfast the next morning, knowing that she'd taken hard earned $$$ from my parents as Mom was cooking our breakfast?

To Mom's and Dad's credit, after the parenting-session that night, neither of them ever breathed a word of that particular incident again. Their point had been driven home. They sensed my shame, and I felt my failure.

The money spent on the dinner that Mom had prepared the previous night, the gas money for that extra trip into town, the money that had bought the clothes we'd worn to the rink, the time spent laundering and ironing said clothing the next day, and even the unexpected lesson on RACISM and my duty to stand against it, equaled to an expenditure of energy. I surmised that their unrecoverable energy was selflessly expended to provide for us,...and it was no less valuable than Mrs. Q's energy.

Except my parents never attempted to, much less would ever follow through with the idea of "cheating a child."

Ergo, if Mrs. Q., lacking in moral conscience, chose to inflict that type of treatment upon a Black child, what principles was she passing on to her children? How were they treating the Black children in their classrooms? What in the world was being overheard from their parents, or discussed at their dinner table about interacting with Black Americans, or anyone who was not Caucasian?

I'll never know.

What I do know is that I never returned a "cheated" monetary difference to my Mom, or Dad for that matter, again. RACISM had drawn first blood on me, and that memory is deeply etched. Unbeknowst to me at the time, I would later learn that while we must not harbor bitterness or resentment, Time, as it turns out, DOES NOT heal all wounds,...but for your next turn up to bat, it just makes the scars a bit more flexible.

****

When Mom signed us up for the local movie theater's Saturday-Summer-Movie-Matinee, once again the funds were handed to me for responsible dispensation. With gleeful anticipation, my brother and I would flip through the ticket book of Disney animated movies that were slated to be shown every Saturday summer morning. It was "our" relished time for weekend entertainment.

So, each Saturday, after chores were done, we'd carefully separate our perforated tickets and prepare for our cinema excursion, knowing that parents all over town would be depositing their kids at the same theater entrance for two full hours of snack-stuffing-animated-thrills-summer-what-took-you-so-long-to-get-here-FUN!

(Now that I reminisce about it, God bless those cinema employees who had a lobby full of kids waiting in line for popcorn, soda, icees, jellybeans, chocolate raisins, caramel, and candy bars.)

When Mom funded me for the movie theater, I was clear that my task was to handle it properly, and to speak out if I felt otherwise. At the ticket booth and the concessions counter, I learned to immediately check and double check the money returned to me *without fear of reprisal or threatening glances if I had to respectfully disagree.* As it turned out, all I ended up having to say was, "Thank you so much!", and that's as it should've been. I didn't get, or let myself be, cheated. I placed the money securely in my romper pocket.

I handed my brother his popcorn and soda, grabbed my concessions and happily turned to navigate our way across the lobby into the dimly lit theater to claim our seats.

I relished knowing that not one extra red cent was paid to become ensconced in whatever intrepid heroines, gallant knights and malicious villains that Disney had crafted for us. The great part?...I didn't spend time fretting that I'd been taken advantage of and had lacked the mettle to correct it. Even better, when Mom pulled up to the curb to pick us up, I confidently returned her monetary change,...in full.

◇ CHAPTER 4 ◇

'He seems nice enough.' The store clerk looked me in the eye and welcomed me as I entered the store. I'd been waiting for this all week. It was my new favorite purse brand, and I'd decided earlier in the week that Friday, after work, I'd go shopping for a couple of new totes. My current oversize purses from another brand had run their course and I'd mentally reached past the point of pre-buyer's remorse, so now was as good a time as any to replace them.

I'm not a compulsive shopper, never have been. So, by the time I decide to "buy" something, I'm usually well past the stage of "needing" something,...and I really "needed" some new totes. All in all, I was feeling profoundly blessed to walk in there on purpose with a plan in mind, ready to "oooh and aaah" my way through my shopping experience. After smiling and returning a greeting to the store clerk, I leisurely set about the welcome task of scoping out colors, styles, new items and oh yes,..."What's on clearance?" As I'm picking up what I like and moving from one section to another, I sensed someone near me.

"Can I hold these for you while you shop, Miss?" the clerk who'd greeted me a few minutes ago asked.

"Thanks, but I'm fine. I'm just comparing and contrasting as I go," I countered politely.

I suppose I could've just chalked it up to boredom, the store wasn't full per se, but I noticed him surreptitiously migrating to whatever section I happened to be perusing. He spoke again a few minutes later, asking if he could help me find something. I courteously refused, and this time I looked around the store and noticed he wasn't shadowing the other women in the store who, ironically, were "not" People of Color. (*Goodness gracious! Does he really think I'm going to abscond with this merchandise? Am I being profiled?*)

After a couple more minutes of stealthily watching him from the corner of my right eye, while he coyly kept tabs on me from the corner of his left eye,...I decided to stage a bit of fun.

I strolled slowly, but deliberately to the opposite side of the store, drawing ever closer to the doors with each step. In truth, I'd mentally selected my purchases from the well-made goods I was carrying and knew exactly which items I wanted to return to their original display shelves. Without making eye contact, I saw him "progress" towards the door as well. He genuinely thought I was uncouth and unconscionable enough to literally *steal!*

How sad.

I hovered just long enough near the door to increase his blood pressure until I decided to put this little ruse to an end. I replaced the non-selected items, took my intended purchases to the counter and demurely, but pointedly commented after the cashier's greeting, "Hi. Yes, I found everything that I wanted. You must have had some thefts occur in this store." The non-Black cashier looked at me a bit odd as if I'd caught her off guard, smiled slightly if not a bit nervously, and never really addressed the statement. She proceeded to carefully arrange and wrap my purchases in tissue before placing them in the shopping bag bearing their logo. I paid in cash, bid her a good evening and exited the store knowing that I'd been treated "pleasantly" on the surface, but "observed" differently because of my skin tone.

I wryly thought to myself, *I may be clutching the same easily identifiable brand-name shopping bag as a White counterpart, but just know that the pathways we underwent to obtain them were in no way comparable.*

By all means, it certainly wasn't a new experience at this point in my life, just unwarranted, unappreciated and worn threadbare thin.

◇ CHAPTER 5 ◇

"THE RACISM TALK" is inarguably what any Person of Color will attest to hearing as a child. Just ask them. The answer will be a resounding, "Yes!" Just as HATRED has been passed down and "TALKED" about in many households across this nation, so has what it means to be an African American in this country.

The main fundamentals include understanding that we were not born on an even keel. How could we when slavery, that interlaced demeaning, family-splitting, achingly-cruel, heart-deflating, soul-despairing, breath-stealing vice is our historical cloak of frayed fabric? How could any **race of people** bearing that heritage possibly begin at the START LINE of this **race of life** on equal footing?

Our Heavenly Father gives us our skin tone; albeit, People of Color just get an extra set of rules if you will, an addendum to the original playbook, select bars of melancholy notes to add to the musical score, a distinctively coded language for our instruction manual that all point in the same direction,... admonishments that resurface on auto-pilot throughout our lives.

"The world will always assume that you know less because of your race."

"Being a Person of Color means that you have to work twice as hard to receive half as much credit."

"Your demeanor will always be closely scrutinized and judged with a harsher mindset."

"You must always be cognizant of RACISM; it's unavoidably ubiquitous."

"You must lend your voice to the revelation of injustice."

So, in essence, there's no even playing field from which we are given to launch. It's not our fault; to be truthful, most times it has not been to our advantage in the least. Hence, why do others outside of our race feel that it's a punitive offense? Punishable by slurs, taunts and threats,...Indictable by whips, dogs, and water hoses,... Prosecutable by segregation and systemic racism,...a Verdict worthy of death.

Without a doubt, my parents have shielded their children from the harsher brunts of racism that they've encountered in their lives, not wanting to mar our childhoods with issues too heavy and

28

inappropriate to breach at the dinner table. Although, occasionally during dessert, some incidents would seep out. My Mom relayed the work experience of being referred to by other than her first name by a White male. No, it wasn't a racial slur, but it was neither acceptable nor to her liking.

After letting him slide a couple of times within the context of the conversation, she confidently voiced her displeasure, and in the same breath articulated that her preference was to be addressed by her given name. Immediately, the group he was with supported her defense; problem solved, and crisis avoided. She'd taken the reins to tame the situation. Women of Color are simply not to be trifled with. They've the strength of lionesses, and I've personally witnessed my Mom predatorily bare her teeth, when provoked to do so, on innumerable occasions.

What about their counterparts, you ask? I'm convinced that there is even yet a special, unwritten set of edicts for Black Men. What makes them unique is only they can mentally relay to each other what it means to navigate this life as a Black Man. Not only are they taxed with adeptly clearing their own daily racial hurdles to survive, but their shoulders are weighted with the protection of their families as well. Award nominated actor, life/relationship coach and debut author Dondre' Whitfield's book, _**MALE vs. MAN,**_ is an absolute must-read and explores this very angle. He says that MEN have an obligation, a role-defining duty to cover and shield those who are, what I like to refer to as, 'in their sphere of influence.' He explains that in doing so, REAL MEN create a safe haven for those who share their lives, thus empowering each of them individually. Add on the daily, inescapable reality of being a **Real-Man-while-Black** and the stakes plunge into a deeper well of the bottomless sort.

My Dad, brother and husband, REAL MEN, have all encountered any number of racially charged situations, not all of which I'm privy to, I'm sure. From theft, to destruction of property, to wage disparities, to heated arguments and threats, to BEING DRESSED IN BUSINESS ATTIRE (BADGE IN HAND) ONLY TO BE CHALLENGED OUTSIDE OF THEIR OFFICE BUILDING AT 6:30a.m. BY A KAREN WHO FELT UNCOMFORTABLE, even to the never-so-subtle nuances inside the workspace,...they can all attest that RACISM shouts in a different tenor to Black Men. It bellows to them relentlessly, constantly daring, persistently contesting their very right to honestly attain a desired level of accomplishment. Too often we expect Real Men of Color to shield their households and those within it without quantifying **what that might entail** just for them to make it back home that evening.

(Thank you Jesus, each and every time, for those who do. Amen!)

◇ CHAPTER 6 ◇

*Is **R**ecognizing the **A**nguish of **C**austic **I**nsensitivity and **S**enseless **M**istreatment all there is to be had in this hate-riddled society?*

Dear Lord, I pray not.

(Can I get a witness to shout another Amen?!?!)

The stark reality is that the destructive and deadly talons of that Beastly Fowl of Prey known as RACISM, are embedded so deeply in this country's very soul, that the rivulets of blood and pain flow seemingly unchecked.

SEEMINGLY UNCHECKED,...because I've witnessed the attempts to staunch this generational hemorrhaging of unjustifiable hatred. These interventions if you will, all came from a myriad of races, and not one of them seemed to mind the hue of my skin tone; they just wanted to help because I was a *breathing human being, just like them.*

It began with an angel, Ms. Pamela S., of my Christian School, who was first in line on the honorary roster of wonderfully dedicated teachers and professors that I've been blessed to encounter. Standing at her desk, she ensured that her youngest pupil not only learned to read with confidence, but nurtured her continued love for it as well when she placed me in the hands of Mrs. Marjorie P., another angel on earth.

There was no biased contempt in my principal who picked me up in his arms one Friday morning before school began, and ran with me and my bleeding, busted chin from the playground to his office, which was half-way across the campus, while I ruined his suit, (I'm so sorry Mr. C.), so he could administer First Aid and call my Dad to take me to the hospital, (THANKS DAD!). I saw nothing but compassion in the young, Caucasian ER doctor a short time later, who took one look at 6-year-old me, one look at her Dad who'd just finished 3rd shift, and gently patched me up with 7 stitches.

From educators who've told my parents that they felt I would "defend my corner of the world", to coaches who had to demonstrate "one-more-time" just for me, to supervisors who unselfishly shared their knowledge to advance my status, to erudite mentors who have blessed me with their deportment of grace, to acquaintances who've shared their lives and those of their children with me,...to the elderly, White gentleman who, just the other day, chivalrously held the store door open for me,...**goodness** in this world amongst all races is still alive.

It's still registering a pulse, but why is it so elusive?

The intricacy of it all is that regardless of race, we're here to seed acts of KINDNESS for whomever and wherever it can be sown, not deeds of discord or dissension. **The heinous crimes enacted against Black Americans is the stuff of hellish nightmares!** Generations of cruel, unjust enslavement don't simply occur by happenstance; generations of putrid prejudice, bloody massacres and systemic racial injustice don't either. That level of deplorable HATRED is **taught**.

It's handed down akin to a rite of passage. It's stoked. It's ingrained. It's seared into the hearts of enough White children who grow into White-Privileged adults who either "don't", or "refuse" to learn any differently along the way. Alas, when White parents don't demonstrate respect towards all People of Color, *their children won't learn how to treat everyone with dignity.* Consequently, the macabre strains of the musical composition denoting the unmerited, unparalleled abuse of Black Americans plays on.

Its conductor should snap the baton in half and exit stage left in disgrace.

This centuries old racial brawl for equality has gone well beyond a bruised, bloody and deadly 12 rounds. There's no need to lower the mic to the middle of the ring. Tell the emcee to ensure that his tux gets returned without incident, because clearly no one wins, no split decision from the judges is forthcoming.

There's only one Judge who matters.

There's only one Judge who can heal.

Jesus has provided atonement for our sins and innate shortcomings if we'll just ask Him. Perfection is an aspiration that we're just incapable of achieving; He never asked for perfection, though. He **did,** however, ask us to treat each other humanely.

It was Evil's design to place in the laps of the Black Race the barbarities of slavery, brutal physical attacks, verbal ridicule and countless other racially poisoned atrocities. Collectively, but far from being all inclusive, they nourish that insatiable animal known as Systemic Racism. A System designed for the lifelong oppression of Black Americans.

Whether you wittingly or obliviously mete out racial modes of injustice, or were born into the receiving, unenviable spectrum of it, take some time to ask yourself, "Where did it all start for me?"

"Now I lay me down before I go to sleep,
In a troubled world, I pray the Lord to keep,
Hatred from the Mighty, and the Mighty from the Small,
HEAVEN, HELP US ALL!"

Stevie Wonder, 1970

About the Author:

Janne Jameson has lived in several different states across the country. She immensely enjoys Christian music, reading, baking, and is always ready for a good movie, (snacks at the ready), as long as the chores are done. She resides on the East Coast with her wonderful husband and is forever a self-proclaimed "kid-from-NC-by-way-of-California."

1libraryfan2@gmail.com

Made in the USA
Columbia, SC
21 August 2020

17208400R00024